Unlock Your Unstoppable
Balancing Life, Love, & Longevity

A Compilation by
Reketta C. Wright

Unlock Your Unstoppable: Balancing Life, Love, & Longevity
Copyright © 2018 Reketta C. Wright

All rights reserved. No part of this book may be reproduced, distributed or transmitted in any form by any means, graphics, electronics. Or mechanical, including photocopy, recording, taping, or by any information storage or retrieval system, without permission in writing from the publisher, except in the case of reprints in the context of reviews, quotes, or references.

Published by WriteIt2Life Publishing;
a division of The L.I.F.E Group, Inc.
P.O. Box 619 Trinity, NC 27370
336.701.2083 | www.icoach2life.com

Cover Design | Battle Branding
Editing & Proofreading | Tequita C. Brice, M.Ed.

Printed by IngramSpark
Printed in the United States of America

ISBN: 0998784434
ISBN-13: 978-0-9987844-3-4

DEDICATION

This book is dedicated to people across the world who have experienced challenges in their lives and found the courage to succeed through those difficult moments. My hope for you is that you will continue to be brave, courageous, and unstoppable.

Contents

Acknowledgments vii

Foreword ix

Introduction 11

Pamela Cunningham 13

Danet Watson 23

Jennifer Nowell 31

Keisha Saunders-Waldron 39

Eugénie Nugent 51

Acknowledgments

I would like to thank my Lord and Savior, Jesus Christ, without you I am nothing. I am thankful that you never left me. Thank you for blessing me with gifts to empower and transform lives. I am forever grateful for your pure love, grace, and favor.
To my parents: Pastor Levy Brown, Sr. and Prudie Brown. Your love and support means the world to me. Thank you for always praying for me. Your words of encouragement were always comforting. I am blessed by our relationship. Thanks for teaching me to remain humble and to be a great woman.

My dearest son Daniel Wright, IV. You are full of love and joy. You've taught me so much about myself. You are my greatest accomplishment. It's a joy to be your mother. I love you with everything in me. You are my daily inspiration.

To my brothers: Levy Brown, Jr. and Jonah Brown. I simply love you guys. Thanks for just being there. To my sweet sister-in-love, Elisa Brown. Thanks for your support and loving me.

My Pastor, Dr. Kevin A. Williams. Thank you for your spiritual guidance. Your leadership has been a blessing to my life. I'm appreciative of your constant support and encouragement.

To all of the co-authors who believed in me thank you. I am grateful for your commitment to this project. I pray many blessings over your lives as we are forever connected.

Special thanks to Tequita Brice and WriteIt2LIFE Publishing. You are truly a blessing to my life. Thank you for lending your expertise and helping me bring this collaborative project to life again.

To Marcus and Tammy Battle of Battle Branding, thank you for your great work on this project.

To everyone that will purchase this book, thank you for your support. Thank you for reading our courageous stories.

Foreword

This book in your hands is about vision. It is about learning about the habits, thoughts, and emotions others possess that allow them to overcome and become unstoppable. It is about learning to live life deliberately and ceasing to living life by default. If you have this book in your hands, you are one of the few — one of the special ones who has made a decision to find out what keys they need to unlock the vault to a life full of purpose and joy.

I remember a time when I felt lost, alone, and as if no one in the world really got me. I walked around aimlessly looking for a lover, a career, a friend, an experience — anything that would make me feel whole and connected. There were fleeting moments, but nothing lasting. There was no real joy.

It was not until I went through my own personal journey of loss, that I was truly able to connect with me — the true essence of me. The God part of me. The part of me that is unstoppable. This type of connection is consistent, unconditional, and timeless. The guidance was always there but I was so caught up in my disconnection that I could no longer hear or trust the strength of the warrior inside of me.

Books like this one you are holding in your hand taught me that there is more to live, be, and express. Being connected to strong women like Reketta taught me that I can have flaws and still possess an inner and outer beauty that is simple and yet divinely perfect. Stories like the ones you are about to read caused my faith to grow and allowed me to be the successful woman that I am today.

I am not sure if you, too, have experienced great loss and you are looking for answers, or if you are intentionally trying to find a path to your greatest inspiration. Either way, YOU are here for a reason and you are being guided.

While you are reading this book, you will consider not only how things are but how they could be. You will question your limitations and expand your possibilities. Through the stories of these incredible women, you will realize the power of the unstoppable woman inside of YOU! So, what are you waiting for?

Monica Lewis
International Best Selling Author & Power Alignment Coach

Introduction

There's no easy formula to balancing life, love, and longevity. I was compelled to compile this book due to my own struggles with balance. Society has often taught us that we have to be better in some areas than others. I believe that mastering and developing parts of your life comes with practice, failures, and growth.

Life is curated into experiencing love on some level whether it's experienced with children, friends, family, or a spouse. I deeply believe everyone should experience love on the level that will expose you to having longevity in life. Balance is something that many desire, but may not know how to achieve. Balance is a daily practice of loving yourself enough to say no to the things that do not serve you. Balance is about setting healthy boundaries for yourself and others. I know, it may sound difficult if it's something you have never tried. I personally learned a few years ago that I couldn't be everything to everyone. I experienced a mindset shift and had my own personal breakthrough after experiencing burn out from people and life. From that experience, I promised myself life would be about longevity and balance in various areas of my life.

In this compilation, you will read stories and strategies on how to live an unstoppable life with life, love, and longevity. I encourage you to love yourself enough to make some healthy changes that will cause you to see your life and the world differently. Remember you deserve it and you are worth it.

Pamela Cunningham

I just love mathematics! In the equation $3a + 2 = 8$, the objective is to find what the letter "a" equals. In order to do so, you would start off by subtracting the number 2 from both sides of the equation, which would look a little something like this, $3a + 2-2 = 8-2$. Once you have done your subtraction method on both sides, your equation should be in this form, $3a=6$. The last step is to simply divide the numbers 3 on both sides of the equation to find out what the letter "a" equals, $3a/3=6/3$. Both of the number 3s on the left side of the equation cancel each other out leaving the letter "a" by itself, and on the right side of the equation you must solve the problem 6 divided by 3 which equals 2.

When I was in school, my teacher's rule of thumb was to always go back and check your work to make sure the equation balanced. Therefore, to check the equation to see if it is correct, you would start with the original equation, $3a+2=8$ and replace the letter "a" with the number 2 to look like this, $3(2) + 2=8$.

You would, then, follow the order of operations on the left side of the equation, and multiply the numbers 3 by 2, then add 2 which equals 8. The sum on the left side of the equation is 8 and the total on the right side of the equation is 8, therefore 8 equals 8 (8=8), and your equation is balanced!

The word balance has several different meanings: to poise or arrange, to bring into harmony or proportion, or to arrange so that one set of elements exactly equals another (i.e. mathematical equation). One of the characteristics of being a Libra is that I am balanced, which means I strive to poise, arrange, and bring into harmony or proportion every area of my life. Is it easy to balance? I would be telling a tall tale if I said yes, but, with practice and determination balancing anything becomes more natural. For example, being a wife, mother, and full-time corporate employee comes with its own set of challenges. I'm not sure many people realize just what juggling these titles entails. The question still remains. How do you obtain a proper work – life balance?

My husband and I had been together for a long time before we said those famous words, "I do". However, we soon found out that being married isn't just about those words. In order to keep my sanity, I have learned to do a few things that may be helpful for you as well, in order to maintain balance.

Prayer! Praying is the one of the most important aspects in life, if not the most important. I talk to God daily, sometimes several times a day to get me through my daily tasks. When wearing different hats in life, you have to constantly be in prayer.

My husband and I are on totally different work schedules. His work weeks vary all the time while my work weeks are pretty much standard, so spending quality time with one another can sometimes be difficult. However, we are learning how we can balance more of our time with each other despite our hectic work schedules. On his early nights, we may go for a bike ride or a nice stroll on the neighborhood trail to give us some energy and put some pep in our step. I also volunteer to be his sous chef in the kitchen just so we can be around each other. We may even take a drive through some different neighborhoods and look at some houses just to have a breath of fresh air. I continue to learn everyday how to balance being a good wife and keeping my marriage healthy.

In a marriage, I feel that it is important to have your own personal space. Sometimes, I need time just to be me and enjoy my alone time. Taking a girls trip, going to the movies with a girlfriend, or just having a girls night in gives you time to just be yourself. It is an absolute necessity. Likewise, my husband may go and watch a sports game at a friend's home or take a stroll in a department store to have his alone time. When we take these breaks from each other, it gives us a chance to regroup and rekindle our love for one another to help us stay balanced in our relationship.

Adding motherhood to the balance equation can take you for a loop. Does this sound familiar? "Mom, can I do this?" "Mom, can I go here?" "Mom, can we get this?" My husband and I have a blended family, however, we still have one child under our roof and things tend to get a little hectic. I have to remind our son weekly to make sure his room and bathroom are clean, take out the trash, and pull the trash can and recycle bin around — as if he is hearing these instructions for the first time. Add in having to remind him to make sure his hygiene and school grades are in check. Yes, children do need to be loved, nurtured, and cared for, however, they will see how far they can go to push your buttons.

Essential to parenting is being able to nurture and communicate effectively with your children, but also set boundaries for them. Our son is a teenager, but he still enjoys the attention and affection he gets from me, as do I. Now, I know we can't be everywhere with our children, but just them knowing you care and being consistent in showing affection towards them reassures them of your unconditional love. So, when I feel like I am teetering out of balance as a mother, I do a few different things. I may do some retail therapy, work on some arts and crafts to relieve some stress, or just take a nap. That normally helps me calm my nerves and think about the reasons God has given me the opportunity to embrace motherhood.

My husband and I are both family oriented. He is the youngest of eight siblings and I am the youngest of four siblings. Finding the balance in all the love that needs to go around is important. After working all week and taking care of miscellaneous things, when a break comes sometimes we don't want to be bothered. But, then we both realize family is all we have. Sometimes calling and texting is just not enough. We are all getting older and as the older generation says, "I need to put my eyes on you!" So, it's definitely important to fellowship with your loved ones. Give me my roses while I'm still alive. Whether it's an hour or so visiting family or hosting family visits, we try to see who we can when we can.

At some point in your life you may have said, "I can't wait until I retire." Some things to consider when you do retire are (1) are you going to find a part-time job just to have something to do?, or (2) are you really going to reap the benefits you spent thirty (plus) years working for someone else? I started working in the corporate world at the age of seventeen. I actually had two part-time jobs and was in school full-time. I went to school, work, and completed homework late at night only to get up and be right back at it again the next day. I often wonder how I was able to maintain balance back then jugging everything on my plate? I had chores at home all while maintaining an Honor Roll average and I graduated with Honors in my class.

After my high school graduation, I moved to Raleigh, North Carolina and attended Wake Technical Community College. Once again, I worked two jobs while attending school and received an Associate of Applied Science degree in Computer Information Systems. I maintained my household duties, eventually got involved in church, developed a thriving social life, and endured all the complexities of becoming an adult.

I have learned to balance my work ethics by conquering a few different skills: time management, organization, and prioritization. Being fifteen minutes early is on time for me, on time is late, and ten to fifteen minutes after, don't even bother to show up. I am currently a full-time corporate employee working five days forty hours per week, with a lot of the same tasks and duties I have had since I began working plus a few extra.

One of my biggest pet peeves is being late — for ANYTHING! It is extremely frustrating for me to be late for an appointment, event, or even work. Growing up, my dad left for work super early in the morning. He was my alarm clock. He would always come to say he was about to head out. My mom's work schedule varied, but that didn't stop her from making sure I was on time. Once I went out into the real world, I had to learn how to balance my time to make sure I was being effective in the workplace.

Organization and everything being in its place creates an environment that fosters creativity and consistent work flow. Each day when I leave work, I make sure things are neat and returned to their proper places to alleviate confusion when I arrive the next morning. However, when the cleaning crew comes in, they may turn my monitors around, move the telephone and calculator out of place, but, I quickly adjust things to how they should be and continue on with my day to make sure things flow smoothly.

Prioritize, prioritize, and prioritize! Try saying that three times fast! It took me some time to learn how to prioritize in the workplace, however, when things got out of control, I had to do something to return my life to its respective balance. So, I started making a to-do list on the daily tasks that needed to be done accordingly. I had my mind set for the amount of time I wanted to spend on each task and made sure I completed it before moving to the next task. Believe it or not, it was definitely a stress reliever.

Longevity – now this is a topic we don't talk about. The bible speaks about a man by the name of Methuselah who lived 969 years (Genesis 5:27). Talk about God allowing you to have a long lifespan. I had an aunt believed to have lived to be over 107 years when she passed. Even to live over 100 years old is surely a blessing. In these days and times, we should be thankful every day just for God allowing us to see another day because tomorrow is not promised.

There are scriptures in the Bible explaining why God allowed people to live so long, however, there are some things that we should do on our end to increase our longevity. I know this may sound cliché, but eating a healthy, balanced diet is one of them. Making sure to get in some exercise at least three times a week, even if it's just a thirty-minute walk is another. We have a gym in our neighborhood and a walking trail. There is also a fitness center in the building where I work, so I have no excuse for not being able to work out. Keeping yourself active will help to increase your longevity. Sleep is also essential to your longevity. One thing I don't mind doing is sleeping. My challenge is often finding enough time to sleep. I'm learning to put myself on a schedule to be in the bed at a certain time because I understand sleep must be a priority. The sleep requirement for an adult is at least eight hours. Anything under that, you are putting yourself at risk for all types of disorders and impeding your chances for a long life span. Make sure sleep lands on the top of your priority list.

Life is full of ups and downs. At times it can seem like a roller-coaster. Finding that balance in life, love, and longevity may be a challenge, however, in the famous words of my deceased grandmother, "You better take care of Y-O-U!" I really didn't understand it as a child, but as an adult I understand exactly what she meant. I know we get caught up in the everyday hustle and bustle, yet if you don't find that balance and take care of yourself, who will? So, I encourage you today to be unstoppable in all that you do and make sure you find balance to live well, love hard, and enjoy a long life!

About Pamela

Pamela Cunningham is from a small town in Craven County, North Carolina called Fort Barnwell. She is the youngest of her siblings and they continue to encourage her to fulfill her goal as a writer. She wears many hats, but what keeps her going the most is being a loving wife, mother, and grandmother.

Pamela graduated from West Craven High School with Honors. After graduation, she moved to Raleigh, North Carolina where she attended Wake Technical Community College and received and an Associate of Applied Science in Computer Information Systems in August 2004. Although, she has her degree in computers, she has always enjoyed literature. She always had the passion to write. Whether writing a letter to one of her girlfriends during her adolescent years to currently writing skits, Pamela has recently become a Junior Editor for a local magazine in Knightdale, North Carolina.

Pamela loves when women can empower and share their stories with each other to be a testimony for one another. She would like to encourage women everywhere to remember to keep God first in all that you do because only He can help you achieve the life you most desire. One of her favorite scriptures is Habakkuk 2:2, ESV, "And the Lord answered me: "Write the vision; make it plain on tablets, so he may run who reads it".

For more about Pamela,
visit www.allwritepc.wordpress.com.

Danet Watson

Where do I start. I guess I will with a mission statement: *You can move forward from past hurts and domestic violence.* First, let me tell you how I moved past my domestic violence situation. I was always attracted to tall, light-skinned guys with curly hair. I would not date anyone unless they had curly hair and I had to see a lot of waves and curls. Looking back, I had some *crazy* thinking. As if their hair and skin tone made their character but one of those light-skinned men, tall with curly hair, would later become my husband.

Our relationship started off with verbal abuse. After dating him for six months, somehow I felt like I could change him because he had all the exterior features that I desired. Does this sound familiar? What I've grown to learn is that you can't change anyone but yourself. Once he felt like the verbal abuse was no longer working, it progressed to physical abuse. But there was something inside of me that kept speaking to my spirit. The voice inside of me kept telling me, "you have to get out of this situation. You are better than this!"

Like most abusers, he sensed that I wanted out of the relationship. Numerous times he promised that he would stop the hitting. I grew more and more tired of calling the police and constantly looking over my shoulder just to do simple things like grocery shopping. I got sick and tired of being sick and tired. I finally decided that I no longer wanted to be in the relationship. However, I quickly found out it wasn't easy to get out, so I stayed...

For months I asked myself, "How did my life come to this?" but I realized that I didn't know who I was. I had low self-esteem and I allowed this man who professed to love me so much, to literally brain wash me. He told me that no one would ever love me like he would. He told me that he wanted me to be so fat that no other man would look at me. I was beaten, slapped, kicked, bitten, and degraded in front of my daughter until I finally made a decision to stand up for myself and then I left. I stayed in a shelter for three weeks until my court date.

While I was away, I started thinking about my life and my future and how I felt like God had something bigger for me but I lacked the strength to stay away from my abuser. He told me if I married him he would not abuse me anymore. Wanting to believe he was capable of giving me the love I felt I deserved, he would have to prove it. And just like that, he stopped.

For two months he went without hitting me! During that time, he demonstrated that he was capable of the most loving and kindness I'd ever experienced from him. I thought this was proof that he didn't have to be abusive to me and that all it took was the promise of a long lasting commitment to each other to make that dream a reality. So, I decided to marry him.

We were married at the courthouse by the Justice of Peace. I still remember that day. As I pulled out the ring to put on his finger, it fell to the floor. Most would say that was a warning sign that I should not have married him. Hindsight is also said to always be twenty-twenty.

After being married only two weeks, the abuse started all over again. Where had I gone wrong? As I looked at myself in the mirror I told myself that I deserved better but my low self-esteem kept trying to convince me that I did not. Somehow I had to change the negative talk that kept recycling in my head.

I began to listen to motivational speakers and started quoting scriptures over my life that referenced who God said I am. The more I listened to the motivational speakers and the more scriptures I quoted, the stronger I became. I looked at myself in the mirror and told the person staring back at me that she was beautiful and that she was the daughter of the King. I told myself that I was the head and not the tail and that I was above and not beneath. Once my mind was renewed, I realized I could no longer live with this abuse and things begin to change.

The change started with me. I had to first start loving me! I had to embrace the Word over my life - that I was beautifully and wonderfully made. The final time I was the victim of abuse, I left — and this time for good.

I stayed in a shelter for three weeks until my court date. I continued to pray and ask God to give me wisdom and direction while I waited. I was determined not to go back this time.

The day we appeared in court, he asked me if I wanted to drop the charges. It was an emphatic, "NO!" Once we were in front of the judge, he couldn't control his anger. He stated, in front of the judge, that he was going to kill me! Instead of attempting to plead his case, he was enraged. He yelled obscenities in the court room and called me everything but a holy women of God. As a result, the judge sentenced him up to three years in prison.

I cannot tell you many emotions I felt. I was elated that I finally stood up for myself because I knew I deserved better! That day God reigned in my life! He gave me favor with judge and an opportunity at a new life. I divorced my abuser and I have never looked back. I was determined not to squander my second chance.

I want to encourage some people who may currently be the victim of domestic violence to not give up. You can make it through if you just hold on, speak words of affirmation, and read your Bible!

Your latter days shall be greater than your past. Stay the course and watch God! I am a living testimony of this very fact.

Today, I am walking in deliverance! When you start loving you, you won't tolerate inappropriate behaviors. Pay attention to all the warning signs and don't be distracted by one's outer appearance. Good character is exhibited by honesty, morality, and ethics. Fall in love with God and watch him Bless you. BE UNSTOPPABLE!

About Danet

Danet Watson knows what it means to survive.

For years, she was the victim of domestic violence. After finding herself abused, broken, and lost, Watson fell head first into a downward spiral, silenced by shame and mental anguish. As her insecurities compounded, she became imprisoned by physical suffering and verbal torment. In an effort to mask her damaged spirit, Danet adopted detrimental eating habits that would sentence her to a life of poor health. In the search to repair both her body and soul, she discovered the Total Life Changes product line and experienced a transformative breakthrough. Coupled with deliberate determination, Danet challenged her behaviors and embraced a lifestyle centered on wellness. In addition to rapid weight loss, her personal journey encouraged her to seek out strategies that would improve her emotional well-being. The end result was a rediscovered physique and zeal for life that she wants to encourage others to find.

About Danet

She has now made it her life's mission to assist people in achieving tremendous, long-lasting success. Her ardent desire is to motivate others to change their lives, and reach optimized personal and spiritual health. Her own ability to emerge from the darkness of her past will inspire you to trim your life and reveal your true self!

As an inspirational speaker, Danet's charismatic flare fosters renewed hope in the lives of individuals who've lost it and are unsure of how to get it back. She is available and eager to inspire both small and large audiences towards new paths of wholeness!

For more about Danet, visit www.danetwatson.com

JENNIFER NOWELL

I was born the 5th of July, a summer baby to teenage parents. Growing up, I was always quiet, shy, and in my own world. I was the one who would sit back and observe other people behaviors. Now, don't get me wrong, I loved to laugh and play — once I warmed up to a person. I was a sweet, loveable, and outgoing child in my adolescent years. I was a silly child who loved to laugh. I always thought laughter to be food for the soul. If you are feeling down, all it takes is to think of something funny to brighten your day or lift your spirit.

For fifteen years, I was the only child on my mother's side of my family. When I was in the ninth grade, my mother remarried and had my brother shortly after. I was active with the dance team and worked hard in school. Being from small town Athens, Georgia, I knew early on that I wanted to experience big city living. My plan was to go to college, get a good job, and live that city girl dream.

My mother was my motivation. She wanted me to

succeed in every way. However, my grandmother was my hero because she believed in me and my dreams. My mother has been my number one fan since the day I was born and my grandmother always encouraged me to believe in myself. Those two women have been my cheerleading squad and always told me "to keep my eyes on the prize." Most of my peers in high school did not finish. They either dropped out or had children. They certainly did not pursue college as their next level in life, so I had the task to stay focused on completing high school.

My high school guidance counselor started my career path my freshman year in high school. She suggested I plan ahead and begin deciding which colleges and universities I might have been interested in attending. I followed her lead and began to plan for my future. To enhance my academic portfolio, I got involved in extra-curricular activities. My hard work paid off. On May 23, 2002, I marched across the stage, and received my High School Diploma from Cedar Shoals High School. There was no stopping me.

With a plan for success in hand, I attended Gainesville College for Nursing. Knowing that I wanted to help our society to have better health knowledge while taking care of them, I majored in Nursing. However, it wasn't quite the experience I was looking for, so I transferred to South Carolina State University. I knew just enough about the school from a family member who previously attended to know this would be the place for me. I enrolled in the Spring of 2004. Quickly my classes proved to be more challenging than I had anticipated and I began to struggle with the nursing curriculum. I knew that I could still help people in life become well, I would just have to go about it a different way.

I thought I had my life figured out. I wanted to be a nurse and major in Nursing, but when I couldn't pass those initial classes, I started to second guess myself. I switched my major from Nursing to Psychology because I still wanted to help people. I knew that was my calling. With that hurdle cleared, I experienced some stability in my life until January 2007.

That year was a sad year for me. My grandmother who was my hero was diagnosed with cancer. This was very hard on my family because she was the rock that held everyone together. For those few months of being in the hospital with her, I had to resign from school for a semester. Those around the clocks visit changed my outlook on life forever.

My grandmother passed away five months later. My mom and I cleaned her house and stored away her belongings. The pain of her loss sent me into an inexpressible stage of grief and depression because without her, I felt empty. I grieved the entire summer but by fall, I realized had to pull myself together. I still had a few classes to compete to obtain my degree. So, I made a decision to take my tragedy and fuel it into positive outcomes.

In May 2008, I graduated with a Bachelor's

Degree in Psychology and was accepted at South Carolina State University into the Master's Program for Rehabilitation Counseling. There were numerous professional educators in my family, from teachers to principals, and they all were more than supportive of my decision to become a counselor. The honesty, empathy, and trustworthiness were the qualities they saw I possessed that would contribute to make me an effective counselor.

Once I completed my Master's degree in the spring of 2010, I thought I had my life figured out. I started working in my career field as a counselor and enjoyed providing various counseling techniques to help individuals build positive relationships. However, internally, I had come to a complete stop. I felt like I had reached a plateau that I didn't want and I couldn't figure out how to get off of it. I had my own relationship problems that kept me feeling stuck and unproductive. I felt like I was giving my all to others but not getting anything in return. I became cold and icy towards people and closed off for fear that I would get hurt again. Normally, I could be very sensitive or considered a softie, however, I put up my defense mechanism and tried to be hard or nonchalant.

I was three years into the workforce post Master's Degree and if my own relationship issues weren't enough, I became frustrated with not making enough money to support myself. Small town Georgia seemed to be closing in on me and I felt like I needed a change. Why not? I was in my late twenties unmarried and with no children. It was time to spread my wings. So, I began to apply for jobs in other states. Just when I was getting excited about the prospect of starting anew in a new place, tragedy hit my family once again.

In October of 2013, my twenty-four year old cousin was a victim of a fatal murder-suicide. She was killed by her boyfriend who committed suicide after he took her life. My heart was broken into more pieces than I can describe because I was not aware that she was dealing with that type of abuse. That situation changed my outlook on life altogether. One day we can be here and the next day we can be gone. The goal being to live your life to the fullest and help someone who is in need.

A month later I moved to Colorado, started a new career, and re-mapped out my life. My thought process was even if the things I wanted did not fall into place exactly as I had envisioned, at least I had a plan. I eventually moved to the Washington, D.C area and that's where I began to thrive. I am currently a PhD candidate pursuing my degree in Human Services with a specialization in Family Strategies Interventions and preparing for my dissertation which will allow me to teach, research, and publish publications to better help our communities. In the meantime, I started my own private practice counseling agency — JN Dimension of Guidance Counseling Services, LLC, and I aspire to develop a non-profit organization for disadvantaged teenagers. My role as a therapist is to listen to people who need assistance. Allowing others to feel your empathy while expressing themselves builds tremendous trust. I find courage in knowing that I can be a blessing to someone through the therapy that gives the client the power to work out their issues and come to a resolve with the techniques that I have learned over the years. This helps individuals to succeed in communicating more openly and freely with their families.

I am a firm believer that prayer works. The relationship I have with God is beautiful. My faith and belief in God has helped me to stay motivated and helped me experience many outcomes that have worked in my favor. I know I was placed on this earth to be a testament for others to never give up even when times get hard. As a leader, I am focused on making changes necessary to help those who need me. Through self-evaluation, I can utilize what I have been through to better work with others and learn them as well. I feel that God has provided me so many opportunities to guide others in his name. In no way, shape, or form am I perfect. Along this journey to success, I know that I will still make mistakes, however, I have the will and tenacity to fight through each obstacle to complete my course. The ups and downs have molded me into the woman I am and prepared me greater. This is how I have balanced my life, love, and longevity. I am unstoppable!

About Jennifer

Jennifer Nowell hails from Athens, Georgia. As a two time graduate from South Carolina State University, Jennifer earned her Bachelor's in Psychology and Master's in Rehabilitation Counseling. She is currently a Doctoral student in Human Service with a specialization in Family Intervention Strategies at Walden University.

Jennifer is a highly experienced Certified Rehabilitation Counselor and Licensed Professional Counselor. She is a mental health professional with over seven years of experience working with a plethora of populations in various settings. She provides individual, marriage and family counseling, and group counseling. She is a counselor and therapist with the U.S. Government and a member of the DC Mental Health Counselor Association.

For more about Jennifer,
visit http://jndimensionsofguidance.squarespace.com

KEISHA SAUNDERS-WALDRON

Just because I am walking through the rain, that does not mean there is not sunshine ahead!

I am the Owner and CEO of Confidential Confessions Counseling Services, where I provide mental health counseling. I am a fierce, confident mom, entrepreneur and wife, but at the end of the day, I am just me! I could start off by telling you all the sorrows and other woes in my life and bringing you into the journey of how I got to be where I am. However, I want to talk about a specific situation in which I dealt with every emotion known to man: frustration, anger, sadness, shame, and happiness, to name a few. What could it be, tragic death, domestic violence, husband cheating, homelessness, victim of rape, you might ask? Although my life has touched on some of these elements whether experienced or witnessed, it is none of these situations. I am not discrediting any of these factors or their significance, however, I want to use this platform to uplift and empower you to be the best version of yourself you can possibly be through my story.

Since birth I have had to face adversity. I was born two pounds eight ounces and only one of two babies that lived out of twenty-three babies in the neonatal intensive care unit that year. I was diagnosed with cerebral palsy and speech problems. I had to learn to walk in a cast and the list could go on and on. When you're met with adversity at such a young age and overcome, you gain a sense of feeling unstoppable. I was told that I was never going to learn like others. I spent time listening to teachers and peers pick on the way I walked and talked. As I got older, I even heard I was not going to graduate high school or college. However, not only did I graduate but I graduated college with a *4.0 grade point average*! So early on I knew how to ignore, tune out, and discredit the naysayers, and press on. This particular situation directly affected five key areas in my life. My physical and mental endurance, social circles, marriage, business, and spiritual beliefs.

One hot summer day in July, I was doing CrossFit® and I was unable to lift the tire and hold myself up like I was accustomed to. Sweating and feeling nauseous, I continued trying to maintain the workout for the next thirty minutes. Not knowing what was going on, I went to lunch with a girlfriend and vividly remember holding my stomach. Holding turned into hitting until I felt like the pain was going to go away but it still lingered there. With an evil stare, my girlfriend asked if I was pregnant to which I responded, "Girl please! Do you know who you are talking to right now?"

In the weeks that followed, my husband and I saw the doctor several times because I was still feeling tired and not fitting in my clothes – they weren't fitting properly. Fitting properly was an understatement. I felt like all the hard work I was putting in in the gym was futile. I was just not seeing any progress, I was gaining weight.

Fast forward to August — the tests confirmed I was pregnant and that is when my story really began. You're probably thinking, "Where is she going with this?" Pregnancy is supposed to be the happiest time of your life. It was anything but that for me. I was in a crazy space in my career and marriage and when I say crazy, I mean, I did not know whether I wanted to continue working for someone else or continue pursuing starting my own company. With regards to my marriage, we were and still are figuring each other out. I felt a baby at this juncture was going to put a halt to that process at a time we were still processing ourselves and individuals and as a couple. I had been living my life not having any responsibilities and married but not taking that as seriously as I should have. Honestly, we were both selfish individuals – too selfish to bring a child into the equation.

When we were presented with the news, I was initially shocked, stunned, and downright upset. I was so deep in selfish thoughts and overwhelmed with anxiety that some days I pretended that it was not even happening! I thought if I continued to pretend, I could continue to travel and live life like I was accustomed to doing. Unbeknown to me the extent just how much that was all about to change.

The first six weeks of pregnancy, I was excruciatingly sick. I cried every day while going back and forth to the bathroom, hoping, praying, and even bargaining with God to please make my morning sickness subside. I threw up so much, I had to be hospitalized four times for severe dehydration. I lost time from work and had even less time for myself. I was still contemplating, "Do I really want a child right now?" This was just the first six weeks. I thought things would get better after the first trimester. Unfortunately, the next thirty-two weeks left me in the same predicament! I remember clearly one incident when running to the bathroom. I did not make it and chicken noodles were on the floor and all up the wall. I was yelling for my husband who was asleep on the couch, like really! I sobbed to my baby, "Why don't you want me to eat?"

As the months progressed and the sickness remained, my phone stopped ringing. Text messages stopped coming in and some friendships became nonexistent. I became isolated and alone. Not able to describe what was going on with me, I felt, once again, I was being tested and prayed, hopefully, I would pass. My best friends became the porcelain crown toilet seat (for throwing up) and my baby. When I did get conversation from family and friends, all they asked was if I was okay and why did I have to go to the emergency room so much. Feeling that they wouldn't possibly understand, I felt that I had to lie and pretend. As Carrie Underwood says, I spent most days "crying pretty" but there was nothing pretty about what was going on inside of me.

At this point, my thoughts were getting the best of me. I began imagining that people did not want to talk to me. When I called some of my family and friends it seemed as if all calls went directly to voicemail. I perceived that they thought they knew why I was calling - to complain once again. This continued for the duration of the pregnancy. I was suffering through so much pain that I did not think I could make it. There were many days I thought I just wanted to die. I kept trying to bargain with God. I prayed and promised to do better if He could just please take the burden and pain away from me - (you see, I still thought it was a burden to be ill and to be pregnant).

One morning early, around 5:45 a.m., as I finished hugging my best friend "the toilet", I went on Facebook® and there was a young lady praying live. As I listened to her pray, I went to what I considered my war room. There, in that moment, I prayed and prayed and cried out to God. Almost instantly, I felt renewed. I went from crying to laughing and being filled with unspeakable joy. My son felt it too as he began to kick with joy!

Fast forward to game day with game face on! After three hours and twenty minutes of pushing, I was told I would have to have a C-section. I cried so hard while the nurse was trying to coach me through the information I just received with her pre-programmed spiel, "You're not a failure!" I said, "When did I say I was a failure? But thanks for highlighting the fact this, too, could be a failure on top of everything else I have dealt with in my life!" Yet another time a choice that had to be made was made for me, not by me and I was not happy about it.

Baby Kyle finally arrived with his eyes wide open, ready for the world! I was not supposed to prevail, according to many, and having cerebral palsy, there were those that said I would never birth a child. The love and adoration that I felt at Kyle's entrance into the world was a feeling of triumph over my naysayers.

I spent a week in the hospital watching nurses poke and prod at my baby. There was nothing I could do about the fury that overwhelmed me. I wanted to guard and protect him against all of the hurt and pain. God reminded me to love him despite what was going on with my body and his body. I prayed that God would show me how to raise a Prince into a King in such a complex world. After being in the hospital for a week, it was finally time for my baby and I to go home.

My time home was short lived, though. One week later, I had to report back to the hospital because now

I was unable to use the bathroom. I was unable to do anything with my body from my waist to my toes and the pain was almost unbearable. (Side note - never take something as simple as using the bathroom for granted).

When I returned home again, the stress of being a new mother really began to set in. I felt like Kyle's crying was unbearable. I felt dark, down, and hopeless. I was not formally diagnosed, however, I knew enough to know that I was experiencing symptoms of postpartum depression. I cried everyday over something as simple as not being able to go to the gym. I was challenged standing in the shower with my beautiful hair coming out in patches. I didn't recognize the person I had become. The changes, the changes, there were so many changes. How am I going to balance a baby, a business, physical and emotional wellness, and being a wife?

Five to six months post pregnancy, I began to settle into my new normal. The power of prayer was the catalyst for my transformation. First and foremost, I asked God for help in prioritizing my life. I used scriptures as words of affirmation to facilitate my mental and emotional healing. I felt that I needed to forgive myself first. I thanked Kyle for saving my life and turning my selfishness into selflessness. I forgave the people whom I felt abandoned me throughout my pregnancy and I continued to increase my time in prayer.

Finding balance in my career had it setbacks as

well, however, I persevered through it. Again, the people I thought would help me the most, have my back, and be the most supportive, turned out to be the most negative and unsupportive ever. One of my mentors asked, "How are you going to juggle being a mom and running a practice?" He then said, "Call me when you're serious." Really!!! I was infuriated. At that moment, I made a declaration. I said, "I will be able to balance my life as a mom and an entrepreneur. People do it very successfully every day and I will be successful too!"

Society and culture norms have challenged the duality of mothers having careers since men came home from war and the women had to hold down jobs and take care of the family. Why should women have to choose? I say we do not. More importantly, I will not. Kyle will motivate me to work harder than I ever have because now someone else is counting on me to provide.

To ensure my success, I connected with like-minded people. I discovered that consistency was the key and I found support in others, i.e. my husband, sister, a few friends, and in others things — mommy support group and the gym. I asked God to renew my mindset and give me strength that I had lost.

At first the transition was extremely difficult. I felt very guilty about leaving Kyle at daycare. However, I can say I am finding success in my business, I am conquering being a mom — loving every part of it now — and with God's help, I am maturing into my role as a wife. My husband and I have now become stronger than before and we have learned how to parent this wonderful kid. My pregnancy taught me the importance of my marriage and that the love my husband showed me during that time was just a portion of the love that God has for me.

I am learning how to effectively manage my time prioritizing what is and what is not important. Understanding the importance of time has helped me create boundaries for myself and with people. I learned to communicate more effectively through this process and to be more intentional about the words I speak into existence over my life. Despite my perceived thoughts, I learned to better communicate with people, most importantly, my husband. After all, he was my number one support when others were not interested in my happiness.

I have learned that being successful through circumstances, trials, and tribulations is a mindset. To weather your storms, you must be mentally and physically fit. Just because my past helped shape some of the person I am today, I knew that I had the skills and tools to help reshape where I was going and who I was becoming. When you are fed up with being fed up, you will make changes!

When facing obstacles in life I want to share six tips that helped me be more equipped:

1. Increase your spiritual relationship
2. Identify your triggers that prevent you moving forward

3. Increase the positive words you say to and about yourself
4. Surround yourself with a great support system
5. Write down your vision so that you can always have something to remind you to move forwards
6. Effectively set boundaries (i.e. saying no and not feeling guilty about it, and managing your time).

Please know, in life there will always be distractions but how you navigate through them will decide your success or failure. So, I ask, what actions do you know you need to take to be unstoppable balancing life, love, and longevity?

ABOUT KEISHA

Keisha Saunders-Waldron is an accomplished Licensed Professional Counselor Supervisor at Confidential Confessions Counseling Services. She considers herself a "Mental Fitness Coach" who changes an unhealthy state of mind to one that is strong and confident. With thirteen years of experience in the mental health field, she consistently aspires to increase the long-term viability of the mindset of an individual. As such, she has produced healthy, enduring results for high profile clients including an R&B artist, an NFL Football player, Senior Corporate Executives and for all with general counsel.

But more than a professional counselor supervisor, Keisha is a mental health advocate, a mother, wife, and a person who influences people to be better versions of themselves. Her opinion is highly sought after and her counsel is well respected and trusted in the mental health field at large.

For more about Keisha, visit www.cccounsel.me.

Eugénie Nugent

It can be a difficult task trying to create balance for every area of our lives, but since it is impossible to balance everything equally, we each must decide what that balance looks like for us. I am Eugénie Nugent, a mom, mentor, business owner, and ardent learner and student. I live in the spirit of yes! I want, and literally try to do, ALL the things I envision doing! People often tell me that I'm living my best life. I remind them that this is my ONLY life, and I intend to live it to its fullest.

I am a solution-oriented planner and executer by nature. That is why I've been so well equipped to take on the roles of empowerment coach, business mentor, and CEO of My Blooming Biz International – a global personal development company where ambitious, purpose-driven women go to unleash their full potential, step into their greatness, and become the woman they were each born to be – living the empowered woman lifestyle.

For as long as I have known myself, I have

always had a plan. As a little girl, I planned that I was not going to have sex before I left high school (pretty low bar I now know) because I was adamant about completing high school without getting pregnant. In my mind, I knew the only way to ensure that was to refrain from engaging in any form of sexual activity. I got that down and that was successful! Although, it almost wasn't! And it's not what you think!

After high school, I planned to travel the world in my twenties and pursue my first degree. I got a job right after high school and since I'd be needing a lot of money for my traveling excursions, I started doing singing gigs as well. (Yes, I love to sing!) That went pretty well. I was able to travel to multiple countries and cities within countries and complete my degree. This was a very defining time for me.

Next, I planned to start and raise a family in my thirties while completing my second degree. I was successful completing the degree but not so much for the family. You see, up until now I've been doing things pretty much on my own. Having to depend on someone else in order for something to be fulfilled held no guarantees. It's not fully within our control. Long story short, I got off-track and endured a really tough time but with the help of The Most High God and my planning and analytical skills, I was able to bounce back stronger and better than ever before. God is good! No, no, no! God is exceedingly amazing and He is able! If we only look to Him, He will turn our setbacks into our comebacks and our mourning into dancing. That's what He has done for me, and what He will do for you, if you let Him.

As a woman, partner, mom, mentor, and business owner, it can be overwhelming navigating the various responsibilities that are all very important and crucial to my overall success. The only way to fulfill my obligations, maintain my sanity, remain healthy, and thrive, is to decide what's most important to me, what can only be done by me, and what can be done by others all while creating a plan to effect and reflect that. Here is a look at the strategies I've used to ensure my unstoppable remains unlocked while balancing life, love, and the pursuit of longevity.

First, I've defined my non-negotiables — those things I will allow nothing to interfere with and make them happen no matter what! The first thing on my list is self-care. MY MORNINGS ARE MINE! They are slow — no rushing, and they begin with prayer, meditation, and sunrise watching with tea. Then it's on to tennis or swimming (depending on the weather and season) followed by a bath and a fiber-rich breakfast. To make this possible, I've designed a morning and nightly routine which includes going to bed early so that I can get an ample amount of sleep in order for me to function optimally. Next on my list is family time. Evening time is family time. I've carved out and secured daily family time where we have dinner together, talk about our day, laugh out loud playing silly, fun games, and affirming our love and appreciation for, and devotion to each other. Then as we wind down, we pray, and surrender to dreamland.

Secondly, I've created a lifestyle that is conducive to the way I want to live and allows me to flex my flexibility muscle. In addition to doing things at my leisure, I can switch my daily tasks around, including my non-negotiables. Things happen! That's life. Sometimes those things demand that we drop everything and attend to them; urgent and important things such as a family emergency or other things you can decide to let interfere with your routine such as a valuable client or friend emergency. I had a client, who made a mess of her books that were needed for an audit the following day, call me up to please help her fix it and you bet I did! Why? Because she has been a valuable client whose books I have overseen for years, I could not risk losing that extra $3,000 each quarter and out of sync books can be costly when audited. So yes, I bypassed my non-negotiables that morning, however, I was able to get right back on track the following morning — $2,000 richer. Money is not everything but it is a lot! (Don't you mess with my coins! Okay?) Creating the lifestyle I wanted allows me to plan and prioritize what's important to me each day and so should you.

Then, I've outsourced tasks that are important to keep my businesses running smoothly but that I do not necessarily need to be accomplish. Some tasks are best completed by the owner of a business while others can be delegated or outsourced. Anything directly related to my clients, (the front-end), I believe are best handled by me – the owner, and that's what I do. Any portion not directly related to my clients, (the backend), can be done by others, and I take full advantage of that. The key is to setup protocols and institute checks and balances so projects will be completed accordingly and all parties held accountable.

Next, I've delegated those household chores that are super important to keeping everything functional on the home front but that also can be completed by someone other than myself. There is nothing more relaxing and calming than a clean, aromatic home, but as much as I do like it that way, I really do not have the time to make and keep it that way. Thankfully, there are house-cleaning services available for just that! So, house cleaning and laundry are definitely delegated and, depending on current events in our home, grocery shopping is sometimes a goner too. I also, sometimes, use car service instead of driving so I can have the use of my hands to accomplish small tasks such as writing or editing one of my books while traveling.

Finally, I've set clear standards and goals for myself. I've purposed to be so loyal to me and committed to my process that no one can make me abandon them. My unwavering devotion to myself and what I'm working at accomplishing is precisely what keeps me unstoppable!. I realized early on that if I did not respect my time, no one else would. In fact, if you're not mindful of your time, others will mindlessly abuse it. I've also learned that people will take advantage of you, as long as there's an opening to do so.

These are the things I've done to keep me unstoppable while balancing life, love, and the quest for longevity, and while I'm at them, I rely on affirmations to keep me solid. Here are a few affirmations you can adopt:

- My God is supplying all my needs according to His riches in glory.
- God's grace, mercy, and favor encompass me.
- I am surrounded by beautiful guardian angels who were charged to protect and guide me.
- The universe is conspiring in my favor.
- I am constantly being replenished.
- My partner was created just for me and I for him and as such, we are attuned.
- My life is filled with JOY.
- I have a happy, peaceful, loving home.
- I am blessed to be a blessing to others.
- The universe selects my clients and they are perfect for me as I am perfect for them.
- I am mindful of my time, and as such, no one can mindlessly use it.
- Money flows to me and stays with me.
- I am living the empowered woman lifestyle.

How did you feel as you affirmed each? What are some of your affirmations?

Balancing life, love, and aligning ourselves for longevity takes work but if we create that design for our individual lifestyles and institute some discipline, then living a balanced life will be seamless. And that's what I've done in order to unlock my unstoppable while balancing life, love, and my aspiration for longevity. Now, I encourage you to choose to unlock your unstoppable as you embark on your journey!

About Eugénie

Eugénie Nugent aka The Biz Bloom Strategist is the founder and CEO of My Blooming Biz International, a personal development and business mentorship company that empowers women around the globe to take an active role in designing the kind of lifestyle they desire, and harnessing the skills and resources necessary to make their dreams a reality. She facilitates workshops, individual & group coaching, and other trainings to help women make the transition from where they are to where they want to be through her programs - Design Your Dream Lifestyle, Let In Vivacious Energy, WERK Your Money Making Genie, M.A.S.T.E.R Your Finances, and UPPPP Your Genius at My Blooming Biz Academy.

Eugénie started her career in the finance and accounting field where she helped business owners, freelancers, as well as divorced women make sense of their finances and up level their bottom line. She has since added coaching to her repertoire and has attained multiple coaching certifications. She holds a BA in Accounting from CUNY MEC and a BS in Management Information Systems from NYU.

Eugénie has overcome many challenges and used the experiences as a catalyst for effectual, intentional changes in her life, and as tools to help women around the globe. She has experienced firsthand the transformational power of coaching to change the experiences and lifestyles of women. And she strongly believes, that when women are empowered, the world becomes a better place.

For more about Eugénie, visit www.eugenienugent.com
And connect with her on all things social @ MyBloomingBiz

About the Visionary

Reketta C. Wright is a heart centered entrepreneur, licensed therapist, and motivational speaker who has touched the lives of thousands during her career. Reketta is known for her warm presence and personable touch.

Reketta is the owner of Wrights Care Services, a private counseling practice in Greensboro, North Carolina, that serves women and families in emotional healing, recovery, and transformation. She holds a Masters in Rehabilitation Counseling from North Carolina A&T State University and has been successful with creating a brick and mortar healthcare company. She is the author and visionary of the book collaboration entitled Wake, Pray, Slay: A Woman's Guide to Being Unstoppable.

Reketta is the proud mother of Daniel (9). She enjoys motherhood, philanthropy, and business. Reketta is living her life on purpose and is on a mission to empower and encourage others to live an intentional life.

For more about Reketta visit, www.rekettacwright.com.

CONNECT WITH US

If you found this book helpful in any way, we would love it if you would leave a review or feel free to contact any of the authors via the information provided at the end of their stories.

Thank you for your support and remember...
YOU ARE UNSTOPPABLE!

www.ingramcontent.com/pod-product-compliance
Lightning Source LLC
Chambersburg PA
CBHW070739020526
44118CB00035B/1719